IT'S TIME TO EAT PASTA

It's Time to Eat PASTA

Walter the Educator

Silent King Books
A WhichHead Entertainment Imprint

Copyright © 2024 by Walter the Educator

All rights reserved. No part of this book may be reproduced in any manner whatsoever without written per- mission except in the case of brief quotations embodied in critical articles and reviews.

First Printing, 2024

Disclaimer

This book is a literary work; the story is not about specific persons, locations, situations, and/or circumstances unless mentioned in a historical context. Any resemblance to real persons, locations, situations, and/or circumstances is coincidental. This book is for entertainment and informational purposes only. The author and publisher offer this information without warranties expressed or implied. No matter the grounds, neither the author nor the publisher will be accountable for any losses, injuries, or other damages caused by the reader's use of this book. The use of this book acknowledges an understanding and acceptance of this disclaimer.

It's Time to Eat PASTA is a collectible early learning book by Walter the Educator suitable for all ages belonging to Walter the Educator's Time to Eat Book Series. Collect more books at WaltertheEducator.com

USE THE EXTRA SPACE TO TAKE NOTES AND DOCUMENT YOUR MEMORIES

PASTA

It's dinner time, come gather near,

It's Time to Eat

Pasta

A favorite meal is finally here!

It's twisty, twirly, long, or small

Pasta is the best of all!

Spaghetti strands or curly swirls,

Bowtie shapes or tiny pearls.

Every shape is fun to see,

Pasta's made for you and me!

With sauce on top, it's quite the sight

Tomato red or creamy white.

A sprinkle of cheese, just let it rain,

Pasta time is never plain!

Twist your fork, give it a spin,

Wrap the noodles, dive right in.

Take a bite, it's warm and sweet,

Pasta makes the meal complete.

It's Time to Eat

Pasta

Sometimes there's meatballs, round and fun,

Or veggies shining in the sun.

Maybe shrimp or chicken, too,

Pasta pairs with quite a few!

Slurp the noodles, that's okay,

It's how we eat it every day.

The slippery strands just slide around,

With every bite, a happy sound.

Pasta's perfect for family and friends,

A dish so tasty, it never ends.

From Italy's heart to your own plate,

Pasta's a food that's truly great!

Leftovers? Yay! Don't throw it away,

Pasta tastes better the very next day.

It's Time to Eat

Pasta

Reheat it warm, and just like that,

It's ready to go for another chat.

So grab your fork, it's time to start,

Pasta's a dish that warms the heart.

It's twisty, tasty, soft, and neat,

Pasta time is always a treat!

When the bowl is clean and you're all done,

You'll smile and say, "That meal was fun!"

Pasta time is the best, you'll see,

It's Time to Eat

Pasta

A happy meal for you and me!

ABOUT THE CREATOR

Walter the Educator is one of the pseudonyms for Walter Anderson. Formally educated in Chemistry, Business, and Education, he is an educator, an author, a diverse entrepreneur, and he is the son of a disabled war veteran. "Walter the Educator" shares his time between educating and creating. He holds interests and owns several creative projects that entertain, enlighten, enhance, and educate, hoping to inspire and motivate you. Follow, find new works, and stay up to date with Walter the Educator™

at WaltertheEducator.com

www.ingramcontent.com/pod-product-compliance
Lightning Source LLC
LaVergne TN
LVHW052013060526
838201LV00059B/4019